SAMSUNG GALAXY TAB S9
FE USER GUIDE

Unlocking the Full Potential of Your Device
and Exploring Essential Features

AARON P. BONNER

COPYRIGHT

1

TABLE OF CONTENTS

INTRODUCTION

Samsung Galaxy Tab S9 FE User Guide

The Samsung Galaxy Tab S9 FE is a powerful yet affordable tablet that stands out in the mid-range tablet market. Packed with impressive features, this device offers a seamless balance between performance and functionality, making it an ideal choice for students, professionals, and anyone looking for a reliable tablet experience. Whether you need a tablet for entertainment, work, or creative tasks, the Tab S9 FE offers versatility and reliability that meets various needs.

Overview of the Device

The Samsung Galaxy Tab S9 FE was designed with everyday users in mind, offering excellent performance at a more accessible price point compared to its premium counterparts. With a large, 10.9-inch screen, this tablet provides users with a great viewing experience, whether for streaming videos, browsing the web, or working on documents. The vibrant IPS LCD display, coupled with a 90Hz refresh rate, ensures smooth visuals and crisp images, making it a pleasure to use for both entertainment and productivity tasks.

One of the key highlights of the Tab S9 FE is its design. The device is sleek, lightweight, and comfortable to hold, with smooth edges that make it easy to grip for long periods of time. Despite its relatively budget-friendly price tag, the tablet maintains a premium feel with a sturdy build and high-quality materials.

In terms of performance, the Tab S9 FE is powered by the Exynos 1380 processor, coupled with either 6GB or 8GB of RAM, ensuring fast app launches and multitasking capabilities. Whether you're working with multiple tabs open in a browser or running resource-intensive applications, the Tab S9 FE can handle it all without significant lag or slowdown.

Additionally, this tablet features up to 256GB of internal storage, which can be expanded via a microSD card (up to 1TB), making it perfect for users who need plenty of space for apps, photos, videos, and documents. The inclusion of Samsung's One UI software enhances the overall user experience, providing a user-friendly interface that integrates well with other Samsung devices and services.

This device is also equipped with an 8MP rear camera and an 8MP front-facing camera, which offers decent photo and video quality for everyday use. The cameras, while not designed to compete with high-end smartphones, offer solid performance for video calls, social media posts, and casual photography.

The Tab S9 FE also comes with an IP68 rating for water and dust resistance, allowing users to confidently use the tablet in various environments without worrying about accidental splashes or dust exposure. This level of durability is a great benefit for those who require a device that can withstand occasional bumps or spills.

Targeted at both casual users and professionals, the Samsung Galaxy Tab S9 FE is designed for those who need a reliable tablet that does not break the bank. Whether you're a student looking for a tablet to take notes, a creative individual needing a device for drawing and design, or a busy professional who requires a lightweight yet powerful companion, the Tab S9 FE offers the perfect blend of value and functionality.

What's in the Box

When you open the box of the Samsung Galaxy Tab S9 FE, you'll find everything you need to get started right away. Samsung provides all the essential components to ensure you can begin using the tablet as soon as you unpack it. Here's what you can expect to find inside:

- **Samsung Galaxy Tab S9 FE Tablet:** Of course, the main feature of the package is the tablet itself. With its slim profile and high-quality display, this tablet is ready to meet your everyday computing needs.

- **S Pen:** One of the standout features of the Galaxy Tab S9 FE is its compatibility with the S Pen. The S Pen is included in the box, allowing you to take notes, sketch, and draw with precision and ease. The S Pen magnetically attaches to the back of the tablet for easy storage and access.

- **Charging Cable and Adapter:** The tablet comes with a USB-C to USB-C charging cable for fast charging. The package also includes a compatible charging adapter that allows you to charge the tablet efficiently. The tablet supports 45W fast charging, so you can quickly power up and get back to using the device.

- **User Manual and Documentation:** For first-time users, the package includes a user manual that walks you through the basics of setting up and using your new device. It also provides information about the tablet's features, settings, and troubleshooting tips.

- **SIM Ejector Tool (For LTE Version):** If you purchased the LTE version of the Galaxy Tab S9 FE, you'll also find a SIM ejector tool to insert your SIM card, allowing you to use cellular data on the go.

Samsung has ensured that the Tab S9 FE comes with all the necessary accessories to get you started. Whether you're planning to use it for work, study, or entertainment, everything you need is right at your fingertips.

Initial Setup

Once you've unpacked your Samsung Galaxy Tab S9 FE, the next step is to get it set up. The initial setup process is straightforward and user-friendly, guiding you step-by-step to ensure a smooth start. Here's how to set up your tablet for the first time:

1. **Powering On the Tablet:**
   o Press and hold the power button located on the right-hand side of the tablet to turn it on. After a few moments, you'll see the Samsung logo on the screen, indicating that the tablet is booting up.

2. **Language Selection:**

   o Upon powering up, you'll be prompted to select your preferred language. Choose the language you're most comfortable with from the list of available options. This will set the default language for your device.

3. **Connecting to Wi-Fi:**

   o After selecting your language, the next step is to connect to a Wi-Fi network. The device will scan for available networks, and you simply need to choose your Wi-Fi network and enter the password. This step is essential as it allows your tablet to download any necessary updates and connect to the internet for setting up Google and Samsung accounts.

4. **Sign In to Your Google Account:**

   o To make full use of the Tab S9 FE's features, it's important to sign in to your Google account. This will allow you to access the Google Play Store, sync your contacts, calendars, and apps, and use other services like Google Drive and Gmail.

o   If you don't have a Google account, you can create one during this step.

5. **Sign In to Your Samsung Account:**

o   Signing in to your Samsung account will unlock additional features such as Samsung Cloud for backing up your data, Samsung Pay for making secure payments, and Samsung's Find My Mobile feature for locating a lost device.

o   If you don't have a Samsung account, you can also create one here. Having a Samsung account is highly recommended to fully integrate your tablet with Samsung's ecosystem.

6. **Setting Up Security:**

o   The next step in the setup process is securing your device. You can set up a PIN, password, or pattern lock for security. Additionally, you'll be prompted to enable biometric features like fingerprint recognition or facial recognition, which can provide an extra layer of security.

7. **Choosing Additional Settings:**

   o You'll be asked to select additional settings, such as whether you want to enable features like Location Services and whether you want to opt-in for Samsung's personalized data features.

8. **Software and App Updates:**

   o Once the basic setup is complete, your tablet will check for any available software updates. It's important to install these updates to ensure your device is running the latest features and security patches. The update process may take a few minutes, so be patient.

9. **Restoring Data from Backup:**

   o If you're upgrading from an older device, you can restore your apps, contacts, and other data from a previous backup, whether it's from Google or Samsung Cloud.

10. **Personalizing Your Tablet:**

- Finally, you can personalize your tablet by adjusting the display settings, selecting a wallpaper, and setting up shortcuts and widgets that suit your workflow. You can also explore Samsung's One UI, which provides a range of customization options to make the tablet truly yours.

With the initial setup completed, your Samsung Galaxy Tab S9 FE is ready to use. Whether you're diving into productivity tasks, creative projects, or enjoying multimedia entertainment, the tablet is fully equipped to meet your needs.

CHAPTER 1

Getting Started with the Galaxy Tab S9 FE

Welcome to the world of the Samsung Galaxy Tab S9 FE, a tablet that blends power, portability, and performance. Whether you're using it for work, entertainment, or creativity, the Tab S9 FE offers an experience that can be tailored to meet your needs. This chapter will walk you through the essentials of getting started with your new device, ensuring you are equipped to navigate its features, understand its physical components, and manage its power effectively.

Navigating the Home Screen

The Home Screen is your starting point when interacting with your Galaxy Tab S9 FE. It's where you'll launch apps, access widgets, and organize your digital workspace. The layout of the Home Screen is simple, intuitive, and highly customizable, giving you the freedom to personalize the device to suit your workflow and preferences.

The Layout of the Home Screen

When you first power on your Galaxy Tab S9 FE, the Home Screen will appear. It is typically a grid of app icons that are organized in rows and columns. At the bottom of the screen, you will find a **dock**—a fixed row of apps that remain visible no matter what screen you're on. The dock can hold up to four apps, and these are usually your most frequently used apps, providing easy access at all times.

On the top part of the screen, you will find the **notification bar** (also known as the status bar). This area shows important information such as the time, battery status, Wi-Fi signal, Bluetooth connection, and notifications like messages or app alerts.

The App Launcher

To access all the apps installed on your Galaxy Tab S9 FE, swipe up from the bottom of the Home Screen. This will open the **App Drawer**, a vertical list of all your apps arranged alphabetically. From here, you can scroll through your apps, search for specific ones using the search bar at the top, or organize them into folders. You can also tap and hold on any app icon to launch the app or make changes to its settings.

Customizing Shortcuts and Widgets

Your Home Screen and App Launcher can be fully customized to create a layout that works best for you. One of the most powerful customization options available is the ability to add **widgets** to your Home Screen. Widgets are small, interactive elements that display important information or allow you to quickly perform actions without opening an app.

How to Add Widgets:

1. **Long Press on the Home Screen:** Tap and hold any empty space on your Home Screen.

2. **Select Widgets:** Tap on the "Widgets" option from the menu that appears.

3. **Choose a Widget:** Browse through available widgets from different apps installed on your device. For instance, you could add a weather widget, a calendar widget, or a music player widget.

4. **Drag and Drop:** Once you've chosen a widget, drag it to the desired spot on your Home Screen.

You can resize widgets to fit the available space, making it easy to create a personalized, functional layout.

In addition to widgets, you can also customize **shortcuts** on your Home Screen. These shortcuts allow you to perform specific tasks directly from the Home Screen, such as launching the camera, sending a message, or navigating to a specific website. To create shortcuts:

1. **Long Press on an App Icon:** Select the app icon you want to create a shortcut for.

2. **Choose Shortcut Option:** Depending on the app, you may see options like "Add Shortcut" or specific tasks like "Send Message" or "Create Event."

By organizing your apps and widgets to match your daily routine, you'll be able to use your Galaxy Tab S9 FE more efficiently.

Understanding the Buttons and Ports

Knowing the physical components of your Galaxy Tab S9 FE is essential for getting the most out of the device. From buttons to ports, each element is designed to give you maximum control and connectivity. Let's take a closer look at the physical aspects of the tablet.

Buttons

1. **Power Button:** The **power button** is located on the right-hand edge of the device. This button serves multiple functions:

   o **Turning the tablet on/off**: Press and hold the power button to turn the device on or off.

   o **Locking the screen**: Press the power button once to lock the screen and secure the device.

   o **Powering off or restarting**: Press and hold the power button until the power menu appears, where you can choose to restart or turn off the tablet.

2. **Volume Buttons:** Located directly above the power button, the **volume buttons** allow you to adjust the sound level of the device. You can also use these buttons to mute the sound or control the media volume when watching videos or listening to music.

3. **Home Button (If Applicable):** Some Galaxy Tab S9 FE models may still include a physical or virtual **Home button**. If available, this button allows you to quickly return to the Home Screen from any app or menu. On newer models, the Home button is

replaced by gesture-based navigation, such as swiping up to return to the Home Screen.

4. **Fingerprint Sensor:** The **fingerprint sensor** is integrated into the power button or the display itself (depending on the model), allowing you to unlock your tablet securely and quickly. Simply place your registered finger on the sensor to unlock the device.

Ports

1. **USB-C Port:** The **USB-C port** is located at the bottom of the Galaxy Tab S9 FE. This port serves several purposes:

    o **Charging**: Use the USB-C cable included in the box to charge the device quickly and efficiently.

    o **Data Transfer**: Connect your tablet to a computer or other devices using the USB-C port for file transfers.

    o **Accessories**: The USB-C port also supports various accessories, such as external hard drives, keyboards, or USB flash drives (using an appropriate adapter).

2. **Headphone Jack:** Many users still rely on **3.5mm headphone jacks** for wired headphones, and while many tablets have moved away from this port, the Galaxy Tab S9 FE still includes it. You'll find the headphone jack on the top edge of the tablet, allowing you to plug in your wired headphones for an immersive audio experience. If you prefer wireless headphones, the tablet supports Bluetooth connectivity for seamless pairing with Bluetooth audio devices.

3. **MicroSD Card Slot:** The Galaxy Tab S9 FE offers **expandable storage** via a microSD card slot. This is particularly useful for users who need additional storage for photos, videos, apps, and other files. The microSD card slot is located on the top or side edge of the tablet, and it supports cards up to 1TB, providing ample space for all your media and documents.

4. **Speakers:** On either side of the tablet, you will find **stereo speakers** designed to produce high-quality sound for media playback. The placement of these speakers helps ensure a more immersive audio

experience when watching movies, playing games, or listening to music.

Camera Placement

The **rear camera** on the Galaxy Tab S9 FE is located in the top-left corner of the back panel. This camera allows you to capture photos and videos with decent quality, perfect for casual snapshots or video calls. The camera is equipped with features like **autofocus** and **HDR**, allowing you to capture clear, vibrant photos in different lighting conditions.

The **front-facing camera** is located on the upper bezel, centered above the display. This camera is perfect for selfies, video chats, and conference calls. It is designed to capture sharp, clear images for your daily communication needs.

Battery Life and Charging

Your Galaxy Tab S9 FE is designed with a powerful battery to last throughout the day, even with heavy usage. Understanding how to charge your tablet properly and manage battery life is essential for maximizing its longevity and ensuring you're never left with a dead device when you need it most.

Proper Charging Techniques

Charging your Galaxy Tab S9 FE correctly is crucial for maintaining the health of the battery over time. Here's how to do it properly:

1. **Use the Included USB-C Cable and Adapter:** The tablet comes with a **USB-C to USB-C charging cable** and an **adapter** that supports **45W fast charging**. To charge your device, plug the USB-C cable into the charging port and connect the other end to the power adapter. Plug the adapter into a power outlet.

2. **Charge in Intervals:** It's ideal to charge your tablet when the battery level drops to around 20-30%. Avoid letting the battery go completely empty or staying at 100% for prolonged periods, as this can degrade battery performance over time. Frequent partial charging is better for the health of the battery.

3. **Wireless Charging:** If you have a **wireless charger**, you can simply place your Galaxy Tab S9 FE on the pad to charge without using any cables. The tablet supports **Qi wireless charging**, but note that this method is slower than wired charging.

Fast Charging

One of the standout features of the Galaxy Tab S9 FE is its **fast charging capability**. With the included 45W charger, you can power up your tablet to 50% in just around 30 minutes. This is ideal for when you're in a rush and need a quick charge. Fast charging also reduces the amount of time you need to keep the device plugged in, allowing you to get back to using it sooner.

To use fast charging, make sure you're using the included charger and cable. If you're using a third-party charger, it's important to ensure it supports the correct wattage (at least 45W) to achieve fast charging speeds.

Battery Health Management

Samsung includes a **battery health management feature** that helps extend the overall life of the battery by preventing overcharging. To ensure your battery stays in top condition:

1. **Go to Settings > Device Care**.

2. Tap on **Battery**.

3. Here, you'll find options to monitor battery health and adjust settings such as **power-saving modes** or **screen timeouts**.

Battery health management also allows you to check the **current charge cycle** and the overall capacity of the battery. If you notice that your battery health has significantly declined, it may be time to consider replacing the battery.

Maximizing Battery Life

Here are a few tips to help you extend the battery life of your Galaxy Tab S9 FE:

1. **Enable Battery Saver Mode:** If you need to conserve power, activate **Battery Saver** mode to limit background processes and reduce the screen brightness automatically.

   o **Settings > Device Care > Battery > Power Saving**.

2. **Adjust Screen Brightness:** The screen consumes a lot of power, so dimming the screen brightness or enabling **Auto-Brightness** will help extend battery life.

3. **Close Unused Apps:** When you're done using apps, make sure to close them, as they can continue to run in the background and drain your battery.

4. **Disable Unused Features:** Turn off features like **Bluetooth**, **Wi-Fi**, and **Location Services** when you're not using them to prevent unnecessary power consumption.

By now, you should have a solid understanding of how to navigate the Home Screen, familiarize yourself with the physical buttons and ports, and effectively manage the charging and battery life of your Samsung Galaxy Tab S9 FE. These essential steps are key to maximizing your tablet's functionality and performance, ensuring you get the most out of your new device. Whether you're using it for work, study, or entertainment, your Galaxy Tab S9 FE is equipped to meet all your needs. Enjoy exploring its features and customizing it to fit your lifestyle!

CHAPTER 2

Display and Customization on the Samsung Galaxy Tab S9 FE

The **Samsung Galaxy Tab S9 FE** comes equipped with a high-quality display that is perfect for reading, gaming, productivity, and entertainment. Customizing the display settings allows you to tailor the tablet's visual experience to your preferences, whether you are looking for a sharper image, a more comfortable reading experience, or smoother gaming performance. In this section, we will explore how to optimize the display, adjust brightness and resolution, and enable features like **blue light filter**, **90Hz refresh rate**, **adaptive display**, and **Night Mode**. Additionally, we will guide you on how to customize the tablet's **themes**, **wallpapers**, and **font sizes** for a more personalized experience.

Display Settings: Optimizing for Reading, Gaming, and Productivity

The **Samsung Galaxy Tab S9 FE** boasts a **crystal-clear display** that is both vibrant and versatile, designed to adapt to various tasks, from gaming to professional use.

Customizing the display settings ensures that the screen performs at its best for your specific needs.

Adjusting Brightness

The **brightness** setting controls how bright the screen is, which impacts visibility in different lighting conditions and battery life. Adjusting brightness to suit your environment is crucial, as too much brightness can drain the battery quickly, while too little can make it difficult to view content in bright environments.

How to Adjust Brightness:

1. **Swipe Down for Quick Settings:**

   o   Swipe down from the top of the screen to reveal the **Quick Settings** menu.

2. **Adjust the Brightness Slider:**

   o   In the Quick Settings menu, you will see a **brightness slider**. Drag the slider left or right to decrease or increase the brightness level. For optimal battery performance, adjust the brightness to a level where the screen is comfortably visible but not unnecessarily bright.

3. **Automatic Brightness (Adaptive Brightness):**

   o If you prefer the tablet to adjust the brightness automatically based on your environment, toggle on **Adaptive Brightness**. This feature uses sensors to adjust the brightness level depending on the light conditions around you.

Adjusting Screen Resolution

The **screen resolution** determines how sharp and detailed the images and text on your tablet appear. The Galaxy Tab S9 FE offers various resolution options to balance **battery life** and **display quality**. Higher resolutions provide sharper details but can consume more power.

How to Adjust Screen Resolution:

1. **Open Settings:**

   o Go to **Settings** by tapping the gear icon from your Home Screen.

2. **Navigate to Display:**

   o Scroll down and tap **Display**.

3. **Select Screen Resolution:**

   o Under the **Display** settings, tap **Screen Resolution**. Here, you will have the option to choose from different settings:

     - **HD+ (1520 x 1080 pixels)**: For a balanced experience between power efficiency and image quality.

     - **FHD+ (2220 x 1080 pixels)**: For high-definition viewing that offers excellent image quality.

     - **WQXGA (2560 x 1600 pixels)**: The highest resolution setting for a sharp and detailed display. Ideal for watching movies, gaming, and productivity tasks that require precision.

4. **Choose the Desired Resolution:**

   o Select the resolution that suits your needs. Keep in mind that **higher resolutions** may drain the battery faster, so consider adjusting the resolution based on your current task and available battery.

29

Activating the Blue Light Filter

Blue light emitted from the screen can cause eye strain, especially after prolonged use. This blue light is particularly disruptive to sleep patterns, as it affects the production of melatonin, the hormone that regulates sleep. **Samsung Galaxy Tab S9 FE** includes a built-in **blue light filter** that reduces blue light emissions, making the screen easier on the eyes and helping to improve your overall viewing experience.

How to Enable the Blue Light Filter:

1. **Open Quick Settings:**

   o Swipe down from the top of the screen to open the **Quick Settings** menu.

2. **Activate Blue Light Filter:**

   o In the Quick Settings panel, find and tap on the **Blue Light Filter** icon (it looks like a moon or lightbulb). This will activate the filter and reduce the amount of blue light emitted by the screen.

3. **Customize the Blue Light Filter:**

   o   To further customize the filter, go to **Settings > Display > Eye Comfort Shield**. Here, you can adjust the intensity of the blue light filter and set it to turn on automatically based on the time of day or ambient lighting conditions.

The **blue light filter** is an excellent feature for anyone who spends long hours in front of the screen, helping to prevent eye strain and improve comfort, especially during the evening hours.

Customizing Themes and Wallpapers

Personalization is one of the greatest advantages of owning a Samsung device. The **Galaxy Tab S9 FE** allows you to customize various aspects of its visual appearance, including **themes**, **wallpapers**, and **font sizes**. Customizing these features not only makes your tablet feel more like your own, but it also enhances your overall experience, whether you're using it for work or play.

Changing the Wallpaper

The **wallpaper** is the background image that appears on your tablet's Home Screen and Lock Screen. You can use pre-installed images or your own photos to give the tablet a unique look.

How to Change the Wallpaper:

1. **Tap and Hold the Home Screen:**

    o   On your Home Screen, tap and hold on an empty area. This will open the **Home Screen settings**.

2. **Select Wallpapers:**

    o   Tap **Wallpaper** to view available options. You can choose from:

        ▪   **Gallery**: Select an image or photo from your personal photo gallery.

        ▪   **Wallpaper Services**: Choose from pre-installed Samsung wallpapers or download new ones from the Samsung Themes store.

- **Live Wallpapers**: Choose from a range of animated wallpapers for a dynamic look.

3. **Set the Wallpaper:**

   o Once you've selected the desired image, tap **Set Wallpaper**. You can choose whether to apply it to the **Home Screen, Lock Screen**, or both.

Customizing Themes

Themes control the overall look and feel of your Galaxy Tab S9 FE, including wallpapers, icons, colors, and more. Samsung offers a variety of themes, from minimalistic designs to vibrant ones, that you can use to personalize your device.

How to Change the Theme:

1. **Go to Settings:**

   o Tap the **gear icon** to open **Settings**.

2. **Select Themes:**

o Scroll down and tap on **Themes**. This will open the Samsung **Theme Store**, where you can browse through various available themes.

3. **Browse and Apply a Theme:**

   o Browse through the categories or search for a specific theme. Once you find one you like, tap on it, and then select **Apply**. This will automatically change your device's wallpaper, icons, and color scheme based on the selected theme.

Adjusting Font Size

If you find the text on your tablet too small or too large, you can adjust the font size to better suit your preferences.

How to Adjust Font Size:

1. **Go to Settings:**

   o Tap on the **Settings** icon.

2. **Select Display:**

   o Scroll down and tap on **Display**.

3. **Adjust Font Size:**

    ○   Tap **Font size and style**, then adjust the slider to make the text larger or smaller. You can also select **Bold text** for better readability.

Customizing the **font size** allows you to make reading more comfortable, especially if you have visual impairments or prefer larger text.

Display Features: Enhancing Your Viewing Experience

In addition to the basic display settings, the **Samsung Galaxy Tab S9 FE** offers several advanced display features that enhance your viewing experience. These features optimize everything from refresh rates to color accuracy, ensuring that your tablet provides the best visuals for reading, gaming, or watching videos.

Enabling the 90Hz Refresh Rate

The **90Hz refresh rate** allows for smoother animations and more fluid interactions, especially during tasks such as scrolling through web pages or playing mobile games. This feature significantly improves the visual experience by reducing motion blur and creating a more responsive feel.

How to Enable the 90Hz Refresh Rate:

1. **Open Settings:**

   o Tap on the **gear icon** to open **Settings**.

2. **Select Display:**

   o Scroll down and tap **Display**.

3. **Enable High Refresh Rate:**

   o Under the **Motion smoothness** section, select **High (90Hz)**. This will enable the 90Hz refresh rate for a smoother display experience.

Please note that enabling the **90Hz refresh rate** can use up more battery power, so you may want to switch back to **Standard (60Hz)** when you're looking to conserve battery life.

Adaptive Display

The **Adaptive Display** feature automatically adjusts the display's color and brightness based on the content you're viewing, as well as the ambient lighting conditions. This ensures that colors are vibrant and images are optimized for each task.

How to Enable Adaptive Display:

1. **Go to Settings:**

   o Open **Settings** from the Home Screen.

2. **Select Display:**

   o Tap on **Display**, and then toggle on **Adaptive Display**.

With **Adaptive Display**, your tablet automatically adjusts the color tone, brightness, and saturation to improve visual comfort, whether you're reading, gaming, or watching videos.

Night Mode for Comfortable Viewing

Night Mode, also known as **Dark Mode**, is a popular feature that reduces the amount of bright light emitted from the screen, making it easier on your eyes, especially in low-light conditions.

How to Enable Night Mode:

1. **Swipe Down for Quick Settings:**

   o Swipe down from the top of the screen to access the **Quick Settings** panel.

2. **Tap on the Night Mode Icon:**

   o In the Quick Settings menu, tap the **Night Mode** icon (it looks like a moon). This will instantly enable the feature and change the interface to darker tones.

3. **Set a Schedule:**

   o For automatic activation, go to **Settings > Display > Dark Mode settings**, and set a schedule to turn Night Mode on and off at specific times, such as at sunset and sunrise.

Night Mode reduces eye strain and helps save battery, especially when using your tablet at night or in dark environments.

The **Samsung Galaxy Tab S9 FE** is a highly customizable tablet that offers a range of features to enhance your visual experience. Whether you're adjusting the brightness, changing the wallpaper, enabling the **90Hz refresh rate**, or activating **Night Mode**, these display settings allow you to tailor the tablet to your unique needs and preferences. The flexibility of customizing **themes**, **font size**, and **display features** ensures that you can create a personalized and comfortable experience.

By utilizing these display settings and features, you can optimize your **Samsung Galaxy Tab S9 FE** for various tasks, from reading and gaming to watching movies and working on projects. With a little adjustment and customization, you can unlock the full potential of your device and enjoy an exceptional viewing experience every time you use it.

CHAPTER 3

Using the S Pen with Your Samsung Galaxy Tab S9 FE

The S Pen is one of the standout features of the Samsung Galaxy Tab S9 FE, elevating the tablet experience by offering precision, versatility, and convenience. Whether you're using it for taking notes, sketching artwork, signing documents, or navigating your device with ease, the S Pen transforms how you interact with your tablet. This guide will explore everything you need to know about using the S Pen, from the basic functionalities to advanced features that enhance your productivity and creativity. We'll discuss how to get started with the S Pen, explore its range of features, and offer tips to help you maximize its potential for daily use.

Getting Started with the S Pen

The S Pen is a powerful tool designed to improve your experience with your Samsung Galaxy Tab S9 FE. Whether you're a professional looking for a precise tool for work or a creative individual seeking to draw or sketch, the S Pen provides a seamless experience that makes your tablet feel more like a digital notebook or canvas. It's important to understand the basic features of the S Pen and how to get started with using it.

The Benefits of Using the S Pen

The S Pen offers several advantages that enhance your overall tablet experience:

1. **Precision and Accuracy:** The S Pen provides pinpoint accuracy, allowing you to interact with your tablet more precisely than using your fingers. This is especially beneficial for tasks such as taking detailed notes, editing documents, or drawing.

2. **Natural Writing Experience:** One of the key features of the S Pen is its natural writing feel. It simulates the sensation of using a pen or pencil, providing a tactile response that makes writing or drawing on the tablet feel intuitive. Whether you're jotting down ideas or sketching, the S Pen mimics the experience of using traditional writing instruments.

3. **Increased Productivity:** The S Pen is an excellent tool for improving productivity. Whether you're making quick annotations on documents, drawing diagrams, or signing electronic contracts, the S Pen

allows you to perform these tasks more efficiently and with greater precision. It's also compatible with apps like Microsoft Office, Google Docs, and Adobe Acrobat, enhancing your workflow across different platforms.

4. **Portability:** The S Pen is compact and easy to store. It magnetically attaches to the side of the tablet, ensuring it's always within reach when you need it. Its small size also makes it easy to carry around, so you can use it wherever you go.

5. **Multitasking:** With the S Pen, multitasking becomes even easier. You can use it to quickly access apps, scroll through documents, or annotate screenshots while working on other tasks. Its intuitive functionality allows for efficient work and better time management.

Setting Up the S Pen

When you first receive your Galaxy Tab S9 FE, you'll need to pair the S Pen to your tablet. Fortunately, the setup process is quick and straightforward.

1. **Attach the S Pen to the Magnetic Slot:** To pair the S Pen with your tablet, simply place it on the

designated magnetic slot on the side of the device. The tablet will recognize the S Pen and pair it automatically without requiring manual pairing.

2. **Check the Battery:** The S Pen has a built-in battery, which powers features like Air Actions and Bluetooth connectivity. To check the S Pen's battery level, go to **Settings** > **Advanced Features** > **S Pen** > **S Pen Battery**. If the battery is low, you can charge the S Pen by attaching it to the tablet for a few minutes.

3. **Calibration:** If necessary, calibrate the S Pen by following the instructions in the **S Pen settings** on your tablet. This ensures that the pen's pressure sensitivity and precision are optimized for your writing and drawing tasks.

S Pen Features

The S Pen is much more than just a stylus. With advanced features like Air Actions, quick note-taking, and Screen Off Memo, it offers a range of functionalities that enhance both your creativity and productivity. Let's explore these features in detail.

Air Actions

Air Actions are a standout feature of the S Pen, allowing you to control your tablet without physically touching the screen. Using Bluetooth technology, the S Pen can interact with your device through simple gestures in the air, making it ideal for presentations, media control, and multitasking.

How to Use Air Actions:

1. **Enable Air Actions:** Go to **Settings** > **Advanced Features** > **S Pen** and toggle **Air Actions** to ON.

2. **Performing Air Actions:** To perform an Air Action, simply press and hold the button on the side of the S Pen while making a gesture in the air. Common gestures include:

   - **Swipe Left or Right:** This can be used to navigate between apps or pages.

   - **Swipe Up or Down:** Scroll through content, such as webpages, documents, or photos.

   - **Circle Gesture:** Open the Air Command menu, which gives you quick access to various S Pen features like screen capture, creating a note, or launching specific apps.

- o **Double-Click:** Open the camera or pause/play music, depending on the app you're using.

Air Actions add an extra layer of functionality to your device, making it more efficient for hands-free operation.

Quick Note-Taking

One of the simplest and most useful features of the S Pen is the ability to make quick notes directly on the screen. Whether you need to jot down an idea, create a reminder, or sketch a diagram, the S Pen makes it easy to take notes on the go.

How to Use Quick Note-Taking:

1. **Access the Quick Notes Feature:** When the screen is off, simply remove the S Pen from its magnetic slot, and the **Screen Off Memo** will automatically launch. You can write or draw directly on the screen without unlocking the tablet.

2. **Write and Save Notes:** Once you've written your note, you can save it directly to the **Notes** app or **Samsung Notes**, ensuring it's always available for later use. You can also convert handwritten text to digital text for easier editing and sharing.

3. **Organize Your Notes:** After taking notes, you can organize them into folders within the Samsung Notes app. Use tags or categories to help you easily find and reference your notes when needed.

Screen Off Memo

Screen Off Memo allows you to quickly jot down thoughts, ideas, or reminders without unlocking the tablet or opening any apps. This feature is perfect for when you need to capture an idea in a flash.

How to Use Screen Off Memo:

1. **Remove the S Pen:** Simply remove the S Pen from its magnetic slot while the screen is off, and the **Screen Off Memo** feature will open automatically.

2. **Start Writing:** Use the S Pen to write your notes directly on the screen. You don't need to unlock the tablet or open any apps.

3. **Save the Note:** Once you're finished writing, tap **Save** to store the memo in the Notes app. You can also send it via email or text message.

Advanced S Pen Features

In addition to Air Actions, Quick Note-Taking, and Screen Off Memo, the S Pen includes several advanced features that are perfect for users who want to maximize their productivity and creativity.

1. **S Pen for Drawing and Design:** The S Pen's high-pressure sensitivity allows for detailed drawing and design work. Whether you're using the S Pen for digital art or editing photos in apps like **Photoshop Express** or **Adobe Illustrator**, its precision makes it easier to create intricate details.

2. **Handwriting to Text:** The S Pen can convert handwritten notes to text in various apps like **Samsung Notes**, **Microsoft OneNote**, and others. This feature is especially useful for note-takers who prefer handwriting but need to digitize their content for sharing or editing.

3. **Screen Capture and Annotation:** The S Pen makes it easy to take screenshots and annotate them. Simply press the **S Pen button** and swipe across the screen to capture a screenshot. Once captured, you can use

the S Pen to draw, highlight, or add text to the image before saving or sharing it.

Tips for Productivity with the S Pen

The S Pen is more than just a tool for writing and drawing— it's also a powerful productivity aid that can streamline your workflow and make tasks quicker and easier. Here are some practical tips to help you maximize the S Pen's potential for productivity.

Set Up Reminders and Tasks

The S Pen can be a powerful productivity tool when combined with apps like **Samsung Reminders** or **Google Keep**. With the ability to quickly jot down tasks and create reminders, you'll never forget an important task again.

1. **Quickly Add a Task:**

    o Open **Samsung Reminders** or **Google Keep**.

    o Use the **S Pen** to write your task directly on the screen or add a new note with a specific deadline or reminder.

2. **Use Smart Alerts:** Set up location-based or time-based reminders using the S Pen. For example, if you

need to pick up groceries later in the day, you can set a reminder to notify you when you're near a store.

Use the S Pen for Precise Drawing and Design

For creative professionals or hobbyists, the S Pen provides a powerful tool for drawing and design. Apps like **Autodesk Sketchbook**, **Procreate**, and **Adobe Photoshop Sketch** are fully compatible with the S Pen, allowing for precise, detailed illustrations.

1. **Create Custom Brushes:** In drawing apps like **Procreate** or **Adobe Fresco**, you can create custom brushes to suit your artistic style. Experiment with different textures and effects to enhance your artwork.

2. **Layer Your Designs:** Use the S Pen to create detailed layers in design apps. Whether you're working on a logo or a complex illustration, the S Pen's pressure sensitivity allows you to build up your artwork with layers, providing a more refined final product.

3. **Edit Photos and Videos:** The S Pen is also great for precise editing in apps like **Photoshop Express**. Use it to zoom in on images, adjust details, and make

refinements that would be difficult to achieve with your finger.

Multitask with the S Pen

The S Pen is ideal for multitasking, allowing you to quickly switch between tasks without losing focus. You can use it to switch between apps, annotate documents, or draw while referencing other apps or files.

1. **Use Split-Screen Mode:** The Galaxy Tab S9 FE allows you to use **Split-Screen** mode, enabling you to work in two apps simultaneously. You can use the S Pen in one app while referencing content in the other.

2. **Drag and Drop with S Pen:** In apps that support **drag-and-drop**, you can use the S Pen to quickly move text, images, or files from one app to another. This can help you stay organized and save time when multitasking.

The S Pen is an incredibly versatile tool that can enhance every aspect of your Samsung Galaxy Tab S9 FE experience. From taking notes and making annotations to drawing intricate designs and navigating your device with Air Actions, the S Pen adds a layer of precision and functionality that makes your tablet more productive and creative. By using the features and tips outlined in this guide, you can maximize your efficiency, streamline your workflow, and explore your creative potential in new and exciting ways. Whether you're a student, professional, or artist, the S Pen offers endless possibilities for enhancing your everyday tasks.

CHAPTER 4

Exploring the Camera System of the Samsung Galaxy Tab S9 FE

The camera system of the Samsung Galaxy Tab S9 FE is one of the device's standout features, offering users the ability to capture high-quality photos and videos whether they're documenting their daily life, creating content, or attending virtual meetings. With both a rear-facing 8MP camera and a front-facing 8MP camera, the Galaxy Tab S9 FE offers flexibility and functionality for a variety of photography and videography needs. This chapter will delve into the camera's features, settings, and tips for capturing the best possible photos and videos.

Camera Overview

The Galaxy Tab S9 FE is equipped with two 8MP cameras that are designed to provide clear, vibrant photos and videos. One camera is located on the back of the device (the rear camera), and the other is located on the front (the front-facing camera). These cameras are not only useful for taking pictures but also for video calls, streaming, and various other creative projects.

Rear Camera

The **rear camera** of the Galaxy Tab S9 FE comes with an 8MP resolution. It's capable of capturing detailed photos and videos, making it ideal for everyday photography, landscape shots, and even macro shots if you're close to the subject. The camera is equipped with features such as HDR (High Dynamic Range) for better contrast and color accuracy, along with **scene optimization** to help the device automatically adjust settings based on the scene you're capturing. The camera also supports **burst mode** for capturing rapid sequences of images, making it perfect for action shots or fast-moving subjects.

Switching to the rear camera is simple: just open the Camera app and it defaults to the rear lens. Alternatively, you can manually toggle between the rear and front cameras by tapping the camera icon that appears in the camera viewfinder.

Front-Facing Camera

The **front-facing camera**, also an 8MP lens, is located on the front bezel of the tablet. This camera is primarily used for selfies, video calls, and content creation. The 8MP resolution ensures your images are sharp and vibrant, while the camera's wide-angle capabilities make it great for capturing group selfies or fitting more into the frame during video calls.

Switching between the front and rear cameras is also done through the Camera app, where the interface allows you to quickly toggle between the two cameras with a tap on the camera icon. The front-facing camera has a variety of uses, including:

- **Selfies:** Take clear and crisp selfies, perfect for social media, profiles, or sharing with friends.

- **Video Calls:** More on this later, but the front-facing camera is excellent for smooth and professional video conferencing.

- **Creative Content:** For vloggers, streamers, and content creators, the front camera provides the ideal tool for recording yourself.

Switching Between Cameras

Switching between the front and rear cameras is as easy as tapping the **camera icon** in the top-right or bottom-right corner (depending on your settings) of the screen. When using the camera, simply tap the icon to swap to the opposite camera. This feature is accessible within both photo and

54

video modes, making it incredibly simple to flip between cameras when documenting an event or creating content.

Camera Settings

To ensure the best possible results from your camera, it's important to understand the camera settings available on the Galaxy Tab S9 FE. These settings allow you to customize your shooting experience, whether you're capturing photos, videos, or using the camera for other purposes like augmented reality or time-lapse photography. Let's dive into the settings you'll find within the Camera app.

HDR (High Dynamic Range)

HDR is a critical setting for improving the overall quality of your photos, especially in situations where you're dealing with high-contrast lighting conditions, such as bright skies and dark shadows. HDR works by capturing multiple exposures of the same image and then combining them to create a balanced photo that highlights both the bright and dark areas in a scene.

How to Enable HDR:

1. Open the Camera app.

2. Tap the **settings icon** in the top-left corner of the screen.

3. Scroll down and enable the **HDR** option (this may be labeled as "Auto HDR").

With HDR enabled, your camera will automatically capture photos in HDR mode when it detects high-contrast lighting. You don't have to adjust it manually unless you want to turn it off for specific shots.

Burst Mode

Burst Mode is a setting that allows you to capture multiple photos in rapid succession. This feature is particularly useful for capturing fast-moving subjects or action shots, such as athletes in motion or pets playing. Burst Mode is available in both the rear and front-facing cameras, allowing you to capture sequences of images that you can later choose from.

How to Use Burst Mode:

1. Open the Camera app and switch to **photo mode**.

2. Press and hold the shutter button (the circular button at the bottom of the screen) to activate burst mode.

3. The camera will take several photos in quick succession, and you can release the button when you've captured enough shots.

Once the burst has been taken, you can go into your gallery and select the best shots from the sequence, ensuring you capture the perfect moment.

Scene Optimization

Scene Optimization is a smart feature that automatically adjusts the camera settings based on what you're capturing. It detects specific scenes like **food**, **landscape**, **portrait**, **night**, and **text**, and optimizes the settings for the best possible photo. For example, when you're taking a photo of food, Scene Optimization will adjust the colors to make the food look more vibrant and appealing. It helps ensure that your photos always come out looking great without requiring you to manually tweak the settings.

How to Enable Scene Optimization:

1. Open the Camera app.

2. Tap the **settings icon** in the top-left corner.

3. Scroll to **Scene Optimizer** and toggle it to **On**.

Once enabled, Scene Optimization will automatically adjust the camera settings depending on the type of scene it detects, giving you the best results for various situations.

Other Camera Settings

1. **Timer:** This feature allows you to set a timer so you can be in the shot. You can set the timer for 3, 5, or 10 seconds, giving you time to position yourself before the camera takes the photo.

2. **Grid Lines:** This setting overlays a grid of lines on the screen to help you follow the **rule of thirds** and compose your photos more effectively. It's particularly helpful for landscape or architecture shots.

3. **Manual Focus and Exposure:** For more advanced users, some camera apps (including third-party options) allow you to manually adjust the **focus** and **exposure**. This provides more control over how your images will turn out, particularly in challenging lighting conditions.

Capturing Photos and Videos

Now that we've explored the camera settings, let's look at how to take quality photos and videos with your Samsung

Galaxy Tab S9 FE. Understanding composition, lighting, and editing can make all the difference in how your photos turn out.

Taking Quality Photos

Composition Tips:

- **Rule of Thirds:** The **rule of thirds** suggests that you divide your frame into three horizontal and vertical sections and place the most important elements of the scene along these lines or at their intersections. The **grid lines** feature mentioned earlier can help you achieve this.

- **Leading Lines:** Use natural lines in the scene (like roads, paths, or bridges) to lead the viewer's eye toward the main subject.

- **Framing:** Use objects in the scene to frame your subject. This could be anything from doorways to tree branches that direct attention to your subject.

Lighting Tips:

- **Golden Hour:** The **golden hour** (the hour after sunrise and before sunset) provides soft, warm light that flatters your subject. This is an ideal time for outdoor photography.

- **Avoid Harsh Midday Sun:** Midday sun can cast harsh shadows and create overexposed highlights. If shooting during this time, find some shade or use reflectors to soften the light.

- **Use the Flash Sparingly:** The built-in flash can be useful in low-light conditions, but it often leads to unnatural lighting. When possible, use ambient light or adjust the camera's ISO and exposure settings for better results.

Capturing Videos

Video Quality:

Your Galaxy Tab S9 FE supports full HD video recording, allowing you to capture crisp, clear footage. To record a video, simply switch to **video mode** in the Camera app and tap the **record button**. For smoother footage, keep the camera steady and try to avoid fast movements that can cause blur.

Video Composition:

- **Stabilization:** Try to hold your device as still as possible or use a tripod for more stable footage.

- **Framing:** Similar to photography, make use of the **rule of thirds** and proper framing for video. Avoid cutting off important elements at the edges of the frame.

Editing Videos:

After capturing your video, you can use the built-in **Gallery app** to trim, adjust, and enhance your footage. You can also use third-party video editing apps like **Adobe Premiere Rush** or **Kinemaster** for more advanced editing options.

Front-Facing Camera Tips

The front-facing camera is an essential tool for selfies, video calls, and live streaming. Here are some tips to help you get the best results when using the front-facing camera.

Best Practices for Video Calls

1. **Lighting:** Ensure that you are well-lit from the front. Avoid having a strong light source behind you (such as a window), as this can create a silhouette. Instead,

position yourself near a window or a soft, even light source to brighten your face naturally.

2. **Positioning:** Keep the camera at eye level for a more flattering angle. If you hold the tablet too high or too low, it can distort your appearance and make it harder for others to see you clearly.

3. **Background:** Ensure the background is clean and clutter-free. If you're in a virtual meeting, it's best to have a neutral or professional background. You can also use virtual backgrounds in apps like Zoom if necessary.

4. **Camera Framing:** Keep yourself centered in the frame with your head and shoulders visible. Avoid extreme close-ups, as this can be unflattering and uncomfortable for the viewer.

5. **Sound Quality:** For clearer audio during video calls, ensure that you're in a quiet environment and avoid loud background noise. If possible, use a microphone or headset for better sound quality.

The camera system on the Samsung Galaxy Tab S9 FE is a powerful tool for both photography and video creation. Whether you're capturing high-quality photos with the rear camera, making video calls, or taking selfies with the front-facing camera, the Galaxy Tab S9 FE has all the features you need to create stunning images and videos. By understanding the camera settings, composition tips, and best practices for both photos and videos, you can maximize the potential of your device and capture moments with ease. With its versatile cameras, customizable settings, and ability to shoot in any lighting condition, the Galaxy Tab S9 FE is equipped to help you create professional-quality content and memories.

CHAPTER 5

Connectivity and Networking with the Samsung Galaxy Tab S9 FE

The Samsung Galaxy Tab S9 FE is designed to keep you connected, whether you are working, playing, or simply staying in touch with friends and family. One of the tablet's key strengths is its robust connectivity options, which include seamless access to Wi-Fi networks, Bluetooth devices, and the ability to set up a mobile hotspot. Additionally, the Galaxy Tab S9 FE supports **Samsung DeX**, a unique feature that transforms the tablet into a desktop-like experience, ideal for productivity tasks. In this chapter, we'll cover everything you need to know about connecting to networks, pairing devices, and using Samsung DeX to enhance your workflow.

Wi-Fi and Mobile Hotspot: Connecting and Sharing Internet Access

Staying connected to Wi-Fi is essential in today's world, whether for work, entertainment, or communication. The Galaxy Tab S9 FE allows you to easily connect to Wi-Fi networks, and it also offers the capability to set up a **mobile**

hotspot, allowing you to share your tablet's internet connection with other devices when a Wi-Fi connection is unavailable.

How to Connect to Wi-Fi Networks

Connecting to Wi-Fi on your Galaxy Tab S9 FE is quick and easy. Here's how to do it:

1. **Open the Settings Menu:** Begin by swiping down from the top of the screen to open the notification bar. From there, tap the **gear icon** to access **Settings**. Alternatively, you can open the **Settings** app from the Apps screen.

2. **Access the Wi-Fi Settings:** In the Settings menu, tap on **Connections**. This section will display all the available network options, including Wi-Fi, Bluetooth, and Mobile Hotspot.

3. **Enable Wi-Fi:** Ensure that Wi-Fi is turned on. If it's not, tap the toggle switch next to **Wi-Fi** to turn it on. Your tablet will automatically start scanning for available Wi-Fi networks.

4. **Select a Network:** From the list of available networks, tap the one you wish to connect to. If the

network is secured, you will be prompted to enter the password.

5. **Enter the Password:** Type in the Wi-Fi password and tap **Connect**. Once connected, you will see a Wi-Fi icon appear in the status bar at the top of the screen, indicating that you are connected to the internet.

How to Set Up a Mobile Hotspot

If you're out and about and need to share your tablet's mobile data connection with another device, the Galaxy Tab S9 FE lets you set up a **mobile hotspot**. This feature allows your tablet to act as a router for other devices, such as laptops, smartphones, or other tablets.

Here's how to set up a mobile hotspot:

1. **Open the Settings Menu:** Go to **Settings** by tapping the gear icon in the top-right corner of your screen.

2. **Access the Connections Settings:** Tap on **Connections** and then tap **Mobile Hotspot and Tethering**. This section will allow you to share your mobile data connection with other devices.

3. **Enable Mobile Hotspot:** Tap on **Mobile Hotspot** to turn it on. Once enabled, the tablet will begin broadcasting a Wi-Fi signal that other devices can connect to.

4. **Customize the Hotspot Settings:** You can change the network name (SSID), set a password, and adjust the security type. To do this, tap **Configure Mobile Hotspot**. From here, you can:

   o **Network Name (SSID):** Set a unique name for your hotspot so that others can identify it.

   o **Password:** Set a secure password to prevent unauthorized access.

   o **Security:** Choose between **WPA2 PSK** or **WPA3** security for encryption.

5. **Connect Other Devices:** After setting up your mobile hotspot, other devices can now search for the Wi-Fi network you've just created and connect by entering the password you've set.

Managing Data Usage and Hotspot Settings

While using your tablet as a mobile hotspot, it's important to manage your data usage, especially if your mobile data plan has limited bandwidth. You can monitor how much data you're sharing through the hotspot settings and adjust your data-sharing limits if needed. It's also essential to turn off the mobile hotspot when you're done using it to save battery and prevent unnecessary data consumption.

To disable the hotspot, simply toggle the switch off in the **Mobile Hotspot and Tethering** section of the **Connections** settings.

Bluetooth and NFC: Pairing Devices and Quick File Sharing

The Galaxy Tab S9 FE supports both **Bluetooth** and **NFC** (Near Field Communication) for seamless device pairing and file sharing. These technologies allow you to connect to wireless accessories such as headphones, speakers, smartwatches, and more. Additionally, NFC allows for quick sharing of files between devices.

How to Pair Bluetooth Devices

Bluetooth allows your Galaxy Tab S9 FE to connect wirelessly to a wide range of devices, such as headphones, wireless speakers, keyboards, and even smartwatches. Pairing Bluetooth devices with your tablet is straightforward:

1. **Open the Settings Menu:** Swipe down from the top of the screen to open the notification bar and tap the **gear icon** to go to **Settings**.

2. **Access Bluetooth Settings:** Tap **Connections** and then tap **Bluetooth**. Ensure Bluetooth is turned on by toggling the switch to the ON position.

3. **Make Your Device Discoverable:** Your Galaxy Tab S9 FE will automatically enter discoverable mode, allowing other Bluetooth devices to find it. If you need to connect to a Bluetooth device, ensure that the device is also in pairing mode (check the device's user manual for instructions on how to do this).

4. **Select a Device to Pair:** A list of available Bluetooth devices will appear on the screen. Tap the device you wish to pair with your tablet, and follow any on-screen prompts (e.g., entering a PIN or confirming a pairing code).

5. **Connect and Use:** Once the pairing process is complete, you'll see a confirmation message. The device will now be connected, and you can start using it with your tablet. The Bluetooth icon will

appear in the status bar, indicating that the connection is active.

Bluetooth Audio:

Bluetooth is especially useful for listening to music, podcasts, or making hands-free calls. Pairing Bluetooth headphones or speakers with the Galaxy Tab S9 FE is as simple as pairing any other Bluetooth device. Just connect the headphones or speakers and enjoy high-quality wireless audio.

Using NFC for Quick File Sharing

NFC is a short-range wireless technology that allows for quick file transfers between devices by simply tapping them together. With the Galaxy Tab S9 FE, you can easily share images, videos, contacts, and other files with compatible devices using NFC.

How to Use NFC:

1. **Enable NFC:** To use NFC, you must first enable it on your Galaxy Tab S9 FE. Go to **Settings** > **Connections** > **NFC and Payment** and toggle the NFC switch to ON.

2. **Place the Devices Near Each Other:** To share content via NFC, bring the back of your Galaxy Tab S9 FE close to another device that has NFC enabled. Ensure that both devices are within a few centimeters of each other.

3. **Select the Content to Share:** Open the content (such as a photo or video) that you want to share, then tap the **Share** button and select **NFC** as the sharing method.

4. **Tap to Transfer:** Once both devices are close enough, you'll feel a small vibration or hear a sound, indicating that the transfer is happening. The devices will then automatically initiate the transfer and share the file.

NFC is an excellent method for quickly exchanging files with other smartphones, tablets, or compatible accessories.

Samsung DeX Mode: A Desktop-Like Experience for Productivity

Samsung DeX is a unique feature that transforms your Galaxy Tab S9 FE into a desktop-like experience. With Samsung DeX, you can use your tablet for productivity tasks that would typically require a laptop or desktop computer. It provides a more expansive workspace and allows you to run multiple windows at the same time, similar to a traditional computer interface.

What is Samsung DeX?

Samsung DeX is a feature that lets you turn your tablet into a desktop-like experience, allowing you to run multiple apps in resizable windows, use a mouse and keyboard, and even connect the tablet to an external monitor. This setup is perfect for multitasking, productivity, and professional work.

When you enable DeX mode, the interface changes to a **desktop-style layout** with an app launcher, a taskbar, and the ability to drag and drop files between windows. You can also open **Microsoft Office apps**, **web browsers**, and other productivity tools, making it easier to work on documents, spreadsheets, and presentations.

How to Use Samsung DeX

There are two primary ways to use Samsung DeX on the Galaxy Tab S9 FE: using the **DeX mode** on the tablet's screen or connecting the tablet to an external monitor to use it in full desktop mode.

Using DeX Mode on the Tablet's Screen:

1. **Activate DeX Mode:** Swipe down from the top of the screen to open the notification panel. Look for the **DeX icon** (it looks like a desktop screen) and tap it to activate DeX mode.

2. **Using DeX:** Once activated, the tablet's screen will switch to a desktop-like interface, complete with a taskbar at the bottom, a home button, and an app launcher. You can now open multiple apps in separate windows, resize them, and multitask with ease.

Connecting the Tablet to an External Monitor:

1. **Connect to a Monitor or TV:** Use a **USB-C to HDMI adapter** or a **wireless connection** (via **Samsung's Smart View** or **Miracast**) to connect your Galaxy Tab S9 FE to a monitor or TV. This will mirror the tablet's screen or, in the case of DeX, give you a full desktop experience.

2. **Switch to DeX Mode:** After connecting the tablet to an external display, tap on the **DeX icon** in the notification panel to switch to desktop mode.

3. **Using a Mouse and Keyboard:** For a more desktop-like experience, connect a **Bluetooth keyboard and mouse** or plug in a **USB keyboard and mouse** using a USB-C hub or adapter. This will give you full control over the tablet, allowing you to use it like a laptop.

What Can You Do in Samsung DeX Mode?

1. **Multitask Efficiently:** DeX mode allows you to run multiple apps at once in resizable windows. This is perfect for working on projects, browsing the web, or referencing documents while writing emails or creating presentations.

2. **Run Full-Screen Apps:** You can run apps like **Microsoft Word**, **Excel**, and **PowerPoint** in full-screen mode, giving you a more desktop-like experience for work tasks.

3. **Drag and Drop Files:** Use the drag-and-drop functionality to transfer files between different apps or between the tablet and external storage devices (such as a USB flash drive).

4. **Use a Mouse and Keyboard:** With a Bluetooth mouse and keyboard, you can control your tablet just

like you would with a laptop, making it easier to type documents, navigate the web, or edit spreadsheets.

The Samsung Galaxy Tab S9 FE is equipped with powerful connectivity features that allow you to stay connected, share files, and enhance your productivity in a variety of ways. Whether you're connecting to Wi-Fi, pairing Bluetooth devices, or sharing files via NFC, the tablet makes it easy to stay linked to the people and resources that matter most. Samsung DeX is a standout feature, turning your tablet into a desktop-like workstation, ideal for handling complex tasks, multitasking, and working with productivity apps. With these connectivity and networking tools at your disposal, your Galaxy Tab S9 FE is ready to meet all of your communication, entertainment, and professional needs.

CHAPTER 6

Managing Apps and Storage on the Samsung Galaxy Tab S9 FE

The Samsung Galaxy Tab S9 FE is a powerful tablet designed to boost productivity, creativity, and entertainment. One of its key features is its ability to manage apps and storage efficiently. With so many apps available for download and various features for organizing, managing, and optimizing storage, it's essential to know how to handle these aspects properly. Whether you're downloading new apps, organizing your app icons, or keeping track of storage space, this guide will help you navigate these processes seamlessly.

This chapter covers all the important areas of managing apps and storage on the Galaxy Tab S9 FE. We'll explore how to download and install apps from the **Google Play Store** and **Samsung Galaxy Store**, organize them into folders, and manage your storage space effectively by moving apps to an SD card and clearing cache. Read on to maximize your tablet's capabilities and storage efficiency.

Downloading and Installing Apps

The Samsung Galaxy Tab S9 FE gives you access to a vast library of apps from two primary sources: the **Google Play Store** and the **Samsung Galaxy Store**. Understanding how to download and install apps from these stores and how to manage app permissions is key to getting the most out of your tablet.

How to Download and Install Apps from the Google Play Store

The **Google Play Store** is the official app store for Android devices, and it's where you can find a wide variety of apps, games, entertainment content, and more. Here's how to install apps from the Google Play Store:

1. **Accessing the Google Play Store:**

   o From your Home Screen, locate and tap on the **Google Play Store** icon. If you can't find it, swipe up to open the App Drawer, and you'll see the Play Store icon.

2. **Search for an App:**

   o Once the Play Store is open, tap the search bar at the top of the screen.

o Type the name of the app you want to download or browse categories to find apps that suit your needs.

3. **Select the App:**

o Tap on the app you want to download to view its details, including its description, screenshots, ratings, and user reviews. Ensure that the app is from a trusted developer by looking at the app's ratings and reviews.

4. **Install the App:**

o If you're satisfied with the app's details, tap the **Install** button.

o The app will begin downloading and installing on your tablet automatically. Depending on your internet speed, this process may take a few seconds to a few minutes.

5. **Open the App:**

o Once installed, you can either tap **Open** directly from the Play Store or find the app on your Home Screen or App Drawer and tap to launch it.

Installing Apps from the Samsung Galaxy Store

In addition to the Google Play Store, the **Samsung Galaxy Store** offers a selection of apps that are optimized specifically for Samsung devices. The Galaxy Store is particularly useful for Samsung-exclusive apps and accessories, including the **Samsung Notes** app, **Samsung Health**, and **Samsung Gear** apps. Here's how to install apps from the Galaxy Store:

1. **Accessing the Galaxy Store:**

   o Open the **Galaxy Store** app from your Home Screen or App Drawer. If you can't find it, you can search for it by swiping up to open the App Drawer.

2. **Search for an App:**

   o Once in the Galaxy Store, tap on the **search bar** at the top of the screen to type in the name of the app you want to download, or browse through the categories for apps that interest you.

3. **Select the App:**

   o After finding the app, tap its icon to open the app details page. Here, you can see the app's features, user ratings, and any special promotions or deals.

4. **Install the App:**

   o Tap **Install** to begin the installation process. Once the app is installed, it will appear on your Home Screen or App Drawer.

App Permissions and Settings

When you download an app, it may request certain **permissions** to access features on your tablet, such as your camera, microphone, or location. It's important to understand these permissions and how to manage them.

How to Review App Permissions:

1. **Open Settings:**

   o Go to **Settings** by tapping the gear icon in the top-right corner of the Home Screen.

2. **Select Apps:**

   o   Scroll down and tap **Apps** to see a list of all the apps installed on your device.

3. **Select an App:**

   o   Tap on an app to open its settings. Under the app settings, tap **Permissions** to view and manage the permissions it has requested.

4. **Grant or Deny Permissions:**

   o   For each permission type (such as camera access, microphone access, or location), you can choose whether to grant or deny access to that specific feature. If you have concerns about privacy, it's a good idea to review and restrict unnecessary permissions.

By carefully managing app permissions, you ensure that apps only access the information and features they need, enhancing both privacy and security.

App Organization and Folders

As you install more apps on your Galaxy Tab S9 FE, your Home Screen and App Drawer can become cluttered. Fortunately, Android offers several ways to organize your apps to keep everything neat and easily accessible. Here, we'll cover how to organize apps into folders and use **split-screen mode** for multitasking.

Organizing Apps into Folders

Creating folders is an easy and effective way to keep your apps organized. By grouping similar apps together, you can streamline your Home Screen and reduce clutter. Here's how to create and manage app folders:

1. **Long Press on an App Icon:**

   o   On your Home Screen or in the App Drawer, tap and hold an app icon until a menu appears and the icon begins to wiggle.

2. **Create a Folder:**

   o   While the app icon is in the "wiggling" state, drag it on top of another app icon that you want to group it with. This will create a folder that contains both apps.

3. **Name the Folder:**

   o   The folder will automatically be named based on the apps you've added (e.g., "Social" for social media apps or "Productivity" for work-related apps). Tap the folder name to edit it, and type in a new name if desired.

4. **Add More Apps to the Folder:**

   o While the apps are still in the "wiggling" state, drag more apps into the folder to add them. This helps you create a more organized Home Screen.

5. **Access Apps in a Folder:**

   o To open an app within a folder, simply tap the folder icon, and then tap on the app you wish to use. This method of grouping apps into categories allows you to keep similar apps together for easier access.

6. **Remove Apps from a Folder:**

   o To remove an app from a folder, simply tap and hold the app icon, then drag it out of the folder. The app will remain in the App Drawer or Home Screen but will no longer be in that folder.

Using Split-Screen Mode for Multitasking

Split-screen mode is a highly useful feature that lets you run two apps side by side, enabling multitasking. Whether you're working on a document while referencing a webpage or chatting with a friend while watching a video, split-screen mode allows you to get more done at once. Here's how to use split-screen mode:

1. **Open the First App:**

   o   Start by opening the first app you want to use in split-screen mode. This can be anything from a note-taking app to a web browser or a messaging app.

2. **Activate Recent Apps:**

   o   Tap the **Recent Apps** button (the square icon at the bottom of the screen). This will show all the apps you've recently used.

3. **Select the Second App:**

   o   Find the app you want to use alongside the first app in the Recent Apps view. Tap and hold its icon and select **Open in Split-Screen View** from the menu that appears.

4. **Adjust the Split-Screen Layout:**

   o   After opening both apps in split-screen mode, you can adjust the size of the windows by dragging the divider between them. You can make one app larger or smaller, depending on your needs.

5. **Exiting Split-Screen Mode:**

   o   To exit split-screen mode, drag the divider all the way to the top or bottom of the screen, and one of the apps will close, leaving the other in full-screen mode.

Split-screen mode is especially useful when you need to reference information from one app while working in another. It's perfect for research, composing emails, or viewing multiple documents simultaneously.

Storage Management

The Galaxy Tab S9 FE offers ample storage, but as you download more apps, take more photos, and create more content, storage space can quickly fill up. Managing storage is crucial for ensuring your tablet continues to run smoothly and that you have room for new files. In this section, we'll offer tips for monitoring storage space, moving apps to an SD card, and clearing cache to free up space.

Monitoring Storage Space

To check your tablet's storage usage, you'll want to know how much space is taken up by apps, photos, videos, and other data. Here's how to check your storage usage:

1. **Open Settings:**

   o Tap the **gear icon** on your Home Screen to open **Settings**.

2. **Select Battery and Device Care:**

   o Scroll down to **Battery and Device Care** and tap it. Then, tap **Storage** to see how your storage is being used.

3. **Review Storage Usage:**

   o You will see a breakdown of your storage usage, including categories like **Apps**, **Images**, **Videos**, **Audio**, and **Other files**. This gives you a quick overview of where your storage is being consumed.

Moving Apps to an SD Card

If your tablet has an **SD card slot** (available on certain models), you can move apps and data to the SD card to free up internal storage. Here's how to move apps to the SD card:

1. **Go to Settings:**

   o   Open **Settings** and tap **Apps**.

2. **Select an App to Move:**

   o   Tap on the app you want to move to the SD card. This could be a game, a social media app, or a utility app.

3. **Move to SD Card:**

   o   Tap **Storage** and then select **Change**. Choose **SD Card** as the destination for the app and tap **Move** to transfer the app.

Note that not all apps can be moved to the SD card, as some require internal storage for optimal performance. You may also need to move files like photos, videos, and music manually if you want to free up space.

Clearing Cache to Free Up Space

Apps store temporary files, known as **cached data**, to speed up performance. Over time, this cached data can accumulate and take up a significant amount of storage space. Clearing the cache regularly helps free up space without affecting your important data.

1. **Go to Settings:**

   o Open **Settings** and select **Apps**.

2. **Select an App:**

   o Tap on the app for which you want to clear the cache.

3. **Clear Cache:**

   o Tap **Storage** and then tap **Clear Cache**. This will delete temporary files and free up space.

You can also clear the cache for all apps at once by going to **Settings** > **Device Care** > **Storage** and tapping **Clean Now**.

Managing apps and storage is a key aspect of optimizing the performance and functionality of your Samsung Galaxy Tab S9 FE. By following the steps outlined in this chapter, you can easily download and install apps from the Google Play

Store and Samsung Galaxy Store, organize your apps into folders, and make use of split-screen mode for multitasking. Additionally, by monitoring your tablet's storage, moving apps to an SD card, and regularly clearing cache, you'll ensure that your device continues to run efficiently and has enough space for new apps, files, and content. With these tools and strategies, you can keep your Galaxy Tab S9 FE organized, optimized, and ready for any task.

CHAPTER 7

Security and Privacy Settings on the Samsung Galaxy Tab S9 FE

In an age where our devices store critical personal data, photos, and communications, security and privacy have never been more important. Samsung has equipped the **Galaxy Tab S9 FE** with a variety of advanced security features to help protect your information. These features allow you to control who can access your tablet, safeguard your personal data, and prevent unauthorized users from gaining access to sensitive information. This chapter will guide you through setting up biometrics, managing passwords and lock screens, and utilizing security features like **Find My Device** and **Samsung Knox** to keep your device and data safe.

Setting Up Biometrics

Biometric authentication is one of the most convenient and secure methods for accessing your device. With **fingerprint recognition** and **facial recognition**, you can ensure that only authorized users can unlock your tablet while avoiding the need to remember passwords or PIN codes.

Setting Up Fingerprint Recognition

Fingerprint recognition allows you to unlock your device quickly and securely with just a touch of your finger. It's one of the most secure biometric authentication methods available, as fingerprints are unique to each individual.

How to Set Up Fingerprint Recognition:

1. **Open Settings:**

   o   On your Galaxy Tab S9 FE, swipe down from the top of the screen to open the **notification panel**. Tap the **gear icon** to open **Settings**.

2. **Access Biometrics and Security:**

   o   In the Settings menu, tap on **Biometrics and Security**. This section contains all the security features related to unlocking your device.

3. **Select Fingerprints:**

   o   Under **Biometrics**, tap on **Fingerprints**. If you haven't set up any fingerprints yet, tap **Add Fingerprint** to begin the process.

4. **Register Your Fingerprint:**

o The system will ask you to place your finger on the **fingerprint sensor** (located on the side or under the screen, depending on the device configuration). Follow the on-screen prompts to place your finger on the sensor multiple times. The sensor will scan different parts of your finger to create a detailed fingerprint map.

5. **Set Up Backup Unlock Method:**

o After registering your fingerprint, you'll be asked to set up a backup unlock method, such as a PIN, pattern, or password, in case the fingerprint sensor is unavailable or unresponsive.

6. **Complete Setup:**

o Once the fingerprint is registered and the backup unlock method is set, you're ready to use your fingerprint to unlock your tablet. Simply place your finger on the sensor to unlock the device.

Setting Up Facial Recognition

Facial recognition is another convenient way to unlock your device. It uses the front-facing camera to scan your face and grant access. While facial recognition is fast and convenient, it is generally considered less secure than fingerprint recognition, as it can sometimes be tricked by photos or videos.

How to Set Up Facial Recognition:

1. **Open Settings:**

   o Navigate to **Settings** by swiping down from the top of the screen and tapping the **gear icon**.

2. **Biometrics and Security:**

   o Tap on **Biometrics and Security** in the Settings menu.

3. **Select Face Recognition:**

   o Under **Biometrics**, tap **Face Recognition**. If facial recognition is not set up yet, tap **Add Face** to start the process.

4. **Register Your Face:**

   o Follow the on-screen instructions to position your face within the camera frame. You'll need to move your head slightly so the camera can capture all angles of your face. Keep the front-facing camera at eye level for the most accurate recognition.

5. **Set Up Backup Unlock Method:**

   o Like with fingerprint recognition, you'll be asked to set up a backup unlock method such as a PIN, pattern, or password, in case the facial recognition fails to work in certain conditions (e.g., low lighting).

6. **Complete Setup:**

   o Once your face is registered, you can use it to unlock your tablet by simply looking at the front-facing camera.

Password and Lock Screen Options

While biometric authentication provides a fast and convenient way to access your device, passwords, PINs, and pattern locks offer an additional layer of security. These methods are critical for protecting your tablet in case someone tries to bypass biometric authentication.

Choosing a Strong Password or PIN

A strong password or PIN is essential for protecting your device from unauthorized access. A password should be long, unique, and include a mix of letters, numbers, and special characters. A PIN is easier to use but should still be difficult for someone to guess.

Setting Up a PIN:

1. **Open Settings:**

   o Navigate to **Settings** from your Home Screen.

2. **Access Lock Screen Settings:**

   o Tap **Lock Screen** under the **Biometrics and Security** section.

3. **Select Screen Lock Type:**

   o Tap **Screen Lock Type** to choose a lock type. You will see options such as **Pattern**, **PIN**, **Password**, and **None**.

4. **Set Your PIN:**

    o   Choose **PIN**, and you will be prompted to enter a **4-6 digit PIN**. Enter the PIN and confirm it.

5. **Set Up Backup Unlock Method:**

    o   Once your PIN is set, you'll be asked to choose a secondary unlock method (like **Fingerprint** or **Face Recognition**) to give you more flexibility when unlocking the tablet.

Setting Up a Password:

For additional security, you can opt for a **password** rather than a PIN. A password allows for more complex combinations of letters, numbers, and symbols.

1. **Open Settings:**

    o   Open **Settings** and go to **Biometrics and Security**.

2. **Select Screen Lock Type:**

    o   Tap **Screen Lock Type** and choose **Password**.

3. **Set Your Password:**

   o Enter a strong password consisting of a mix of letters (upper and lowercase), numbers, and special characters. Confirm the password.

4. **Set Up Backup Unlock Method:**

   o As with PIN setup, choose a secondary unlock method, such as **Fingerprint** or **Face Recognition**, for added convenience.

Lock Screen Options:

The lock screen settings allow you to customize how your tablet behaves when locked. You can choose to show or hide notifications, adjust the screen timeout, and enable features like **Always On Display** for quick information access.

Customizing the Lock Screen:

1. **Open Settings:**

   o Tap on **Settings**, then go to **Lock Screen** under the **Biometrics and Security** section.

2. **Lock Screen Features:**

   o From here, you can choose to:

- **Show or hide notifications** on the lock screen.

- **Enable Always On Display** to show useful information like time, date, and notifications even when the device is locked.

- **Change the lock screen wallpaper** and add widgets.

- **Set up shortcuts** for apps, such as the camera or messaging app, to quickly access them from the lock screen.

3. **Choose Screen Timeout:**

   o Tap **Screen Timeout** to choose how long the screen remains active before automatically locking. Options typically range from 15 seconds to 30 minutes, but for security reasons, a shorter timeout (e.g., 1 minute) is recommended.

Protecting Personal Data

Protecting personal data is crucial in today's connected world. The Galaxy Tab S9 FE offers advanced features like

Find My Device and **Samsung Knox** to help secure your personal information and ensure you can track your device in case it's lost or stolen.

Using Find My Device

Find My Device is a feature that helps you locate your tablet if it's lost or misplaced. It allows you to remotely track your device, lock it, or erase all data to prevent unauthorized access.

How to Set Up Find My Device:

1. **Open Settings:**

   o Tap on **Settings**, then go to **Biometrics and Security**.

2. **Enable Find My Device:**

   o Scroll down to **Find My Mobile** and tap on it. If prompted, sign in with your Samsung account. Ensure that **Find My Device** is toggled ON.

3. **Remote Access and Lock:**

   o Once activated, you can remotely track your tablet using the **Find My Mobile** website (findmymobile.samsung.com) or the **Find My Mobile** app on another device.

o You can also remotely lock the device, ring it, or erase all data in case the tablet is lost or stolen.

Find My Device is particularly helpful when you need to locate your tablet or ensure that no one can access your data.

Using Samsung Knox

Samsung Knox is a comprehensive security platform designed to protect both your personal and professional data. It offers features like **secure boot**, **real-time kernel protection**, and **data encryption**, ensuring that your tablet is protected from threats, even when you're using third-party apps or services.

How to Use Samsung Knox:

1. **Access Samsung Knox:**

   o To activate Samsung Knox, open **Settings**, then go to **Biometrics and Security** and select **Samsung Knox**.

   o You may need to sign in with your Samsung account if you haven't done so already.

2. **Secure Your Data:**

    o Samsung Knox offers features such as **Secure Folder**, which lets you create a separate, encrypted space on your tablet to store sensitive data like apps, files, and documents.

    o **Secure Folder** can be locked with a PIN, password, or biometric authentication, ensuring that your sensitive data is protected even if someone gains access to your tablet.

3. **Real-Time Protection:**

    o Samsung Knox constantly monitors your device for security threats, including malware, unauthorized access attempts, and more. It provides real-time protection and alerts you if any suspicious activity is detected.

4. **Enterprise-Level Security:**

    o Samsung Knox is also used in enterprise environments to secure corporate data and applications on mobile devices. It offers features like **containerization**, which keeps

101

personal and work data separate for better security and privacy.

Securing your **Samsung Galaxy Tab S9 FE** is essential to protecting your personal data, whether it's photos, messages, or apps. By setting up biometrics, such as fingerprint and facial recognition, and using secure passwords or PINs, you can ensure that only authorized users have access to your device. Additionally, enabling features like **Find My Device** and **Samsung Knox** enhances your tablet's security and ensures your data stays protected, even in the event of loss or theft. Regularly reviewing and updating your security settings, as well as using advanced features like secure folders and real-time protection, will help safeguard your device and data in the digital age. With these security measures in place, your Galaxy Tab S9 FE will stay secure and private, no matter what challenges come your way.

CHAPTER 8

Performance and Battery Optimization on the Samsung Galaxy Tab S9 FE

The **Samsung Galaxy Tab S9 FE** is a powerful device that delivers excellent performance for a wide variety of tasks, including productivity, entertainment, and gaming. However, like any device, it's important to manage performance and battery life to ensure it runs efficiently and lasts throughout the day. In this chapter, we'll explore how to improve tablet performance by managing apps, clearing cache, and optimizing settings. We'll also cover battery-saving tips to help you extend your tablet's battery life, as well as how to keep your system up to date with software updates to ensure security and smooth performance.

Improving Tablet Performance

Performance optimization is key to ensuring that your **Samsung Galaxy Tab S9 FE** operates at its best, even with numerous apps and files installed. Over time, your tablet may slow down due to background processes, apps running inefficiently, or storage being filled with cached data.

Fortunately, there are several methods you can use to enhance the tablet's speed and performance.

Disabling Unused Apps

One of the primary reasons for a slowdown in device performance is the accumulation of apps that are rarely used but still take up valuable system resources. Disabling unused apps ensures that they do not consume CPU and memory resources in the background, helping your tablet run smoother.

How to Disable Unused Apps:

1. **Open Settings:**

   o From your **Home Screen** or **App Drawer**, tap the **gear icon** to open **Settings**.

2. **Go to Apps:**

   o Scroll down and select **Apps** from the Settings menu. This will display a list of all installed apps on your tablet.

3. **Choose the App to Disable:**

   o Browse through the list of apps and find the ones you want to disable. Tap on the app's name to open its settings.

4. **Disable the App:**

   o If an app cannot be uninstalled (such as pre-installed system apps), you will have the option to **Disable** it instead. Tap the **Disable** button to prevent the app from running in the background. Disabled apps will no longer appear in your App Drawer or consume resources, though you can always re-enable them later.

Benefits of Disabling Apps:

- **Free up system resources** like RAM and CPU, leading to better performance.

- **Reduce battery drain** caused by background processes.

- **Minimize clutter** in your App Drawer, making it easier to navigate your device.

Clearing Cache

Over time, apps accumulate **cached data** that can take up significant storage space and slow down the device. Cached data is stored to help apps load faster, but it can become unnecessary and contribute to system slowdowns if not managed regularly. Clearing the cache is a simple way to free up space and improve the tablet's performance.

How to Clear Cache for Apps:

1. **Open Settings:**

   o From the **Home Screen**, go to **Settings**.

2. **Go to Apps:**

   o Tap on **Apps** and select the app from which you want to clear the cache.

3. **Clear Cache:**

   o In the app's settings, tap on **Storage**, then select **Clear Cache**. This will delete temporary files that are no longer needed but leave your app's data intact.

How to Clear System Cache:

To clear the system cache for the entire device, follow these steps:

1. **Power Off the Tablet:**

   o Power off your Galaxy Tab S9 FE by holding down the **Power** button and selecting **Power Off**.

2. **Enter Recovery Mode:**

   o Press and hold the **Volume Up** and **Power** buttons simultaneously until the Samsung logo appears. Release the buttons to enter **Recovery Mode**.

3. **Clear Cache Partition:**

   o In recovery mode, use the **Volume Down** button to highlight **Wipe Cache Partition** and press **Power** to select it. Confirm the action and wait for the process to complete.

Clearing the cache periodically will help keep your device running efficiently, freeing up storage and reducing unnecessary processes that slow down your tablet.

Optimizing Settings for Speed

There are several system settings on the **Galaxy Tab S9 FE** that can be adjusted to enhance performance, especially when you notice lag or slow response times.

Enable Developer Options for Speed Optimization:

1. **Open Settings:**

   o Go to **Settings** > **About Tablet**.

2. **Activate Developer Options:**

   o Tap on **Software Information** and find the **Build Number**. Tap on the **Build Number** seven times in quick succession. You'll see a message saying **Developer mode has been enabled**.

3. **Optimize Developer Options:**

   o Once Developer Options are enabled, go back to **Settings** and tap **Developer Options** (under **System**). Here, you can make several adjustments:

- **Window Animation Scale**: Reduce the animation scale to 0.5x or turn it off to speed up transitions.

- **Transition Animation Scale**: Similar to window animations, reducing this scale can help improve responsiveness.

- **Background Process Limit**: Limit the number of background processes to optimize performance and prevent resource hogging.

By enabling Developer Options and adjusting these settings, you can make your tablet more responsive and reduce lag during navigation and app usage.

Battery Saving Tips

Battery life is one of the most critical concerns for tablet users. While the **Samsung Galaxy Tab S9 FE** is equipped with a sizable battery, knowing how to conserve energy can help extend battery life throughout the day. There are a variety of **power-saving features** and settings that can minimize battery drain, from reducing background app activity to activating power-saving modes.

Battery Saver Mode

The **Battery Saver Mode** is an easy way to reduce battery consumption by limiting background processes and reducing screen brightness. When enabled, it helps extend battery life, especially when you're running low on power.

How to Enable Battery Saver Mode:

1. **Open Settings:**

   o Swipe down from the top of the screen to open the **notification panel**, and tap the **gear icon** to access **Settings**.

2. **Go to Battery:**

   o Tap on **Battery and Device Care**, then tap **Battery**.

3. **Enable Power Saving Mode:**

   o Tap **Power Saving Mode** to toggle it on. You'll have the option to choose between:

     ▪ **Medium Power Saving**: Reduces CPU speed, limits background apps, and lowers screen brightness.

- **Maximum Power Saving**: Further reduces performance, limits apps, and disables background data.

4. **Activate Power Mode from Quick Settings:**

   o You can also activate **Battery Saver Mode** quickly from the **Quick Settings** panel by swiping down from the top of the screen and tapping the **Battery Saver** icon.

When to Use Battery Saver Mode:

- **During long trips** when you need to conserve power but don't have access to a charger.

- **When your battery is below 20%**, and you want to extend battery life until you can charge the tablet.

- **When you're using low-power apps** and don't need the tablet's full performance.

Reducing Background App Activity

Apps running in the background can be a major drain on battery life. Some apps continue to use data and resources even when you're not actively using them. To reduce battery consumption, it's important to limit unnecessary background activity.

How to Manage Background Apps:

1. **Open Settings:**

   o   Go to **Settings** and tap **Apps**.

2. **Restrict Background Apps:**

   o   For each app, you can go into its settings and tap on **Battery**. You'll have the option to disable **Background Activity** for certain apps, which prevents them from running when not in use.

3. **Use Battery Optimization:**

   o   In the **Battery** settings, you can also enable **Battery Optimization** for individual apps. This feature optimizes battery usage by restricting background processes and limiting excessive resource usage.

4. **Close Unused Apps:**

   o   Regularly close apps that you're not actively using. You can swipe up from the bottom to open the **Recent Apps** menu and swipe away apps to close them.

By reducing background app activity, you can significantly reduce the amount of power your tablet consumes, extending battery life throughout the day.

Updating Software

Keeping your Galaxy Tab S9 FE up to date with the latest software is essential for both performance and security. System updates often include performance improvements, bug fixes, and security patches that ensure your device runs smoothly and securely.

How to Check for and Install System Updates

1. **Open Settings:**

   o Swipe down from the top of the screen and tap the **gear icon** to open **Settings**.

2. **Access Software Update:**

   o Scroll down and tap **Software Update**.

3. **Check for Updates:**

   o Tap **Download and Install** to check for any available updates. If an update is available, your tablet will prompt you to download it.

4. **Install the Update:**

    o   Once the download is complete, you'll be prompted to restart your device to install the update. Ensure your tablet is connected to Wi-Fi and has sufficient battery or is plugged in before proceeding with the installation.

Enable Automatic Updates

To ensure that your tablet is always running the latest software without manually checking for updates, you can enable automatic updates:

1. **Go to Software Update:**

    o   Open **Settings**, tap **Software Update**, and enable **Auto Download Over Wi-Fi**.

2. **Enable Auto Install:**

    o   This setting allows your tablet to automatically download and install updates when connected to Wi-Fi, ensuring that your device is always up to date.

By keeping your tablet updated, you can benefit from the latest features, improved system stability, and enhanced security.

Optimizing the performance and battery life of your Samsung Galaxy Tab S9 FE ensures that it runs smoothly and efficiently, maximizing its potential for all your activities. By following the steps in this chapter, you can manage your device's performance by disabling unused apps, clearing cache, and optimizing settings for speed. Implementing power-saving features like Battery Saver mode, reducing background app activity, and regularly updating software can help extend your tablet's battery life and ensure it remains secure and up-to-date. With these techniques, you can keep your Galaxy Tab S9 FE performing at its best, whether you're using it for work, entertainment, or everything in between.

CHAPTER 9

Troubleshooting and Maintenance on the Samsung Galaxy Tab S9 FE

While the **Samsung Galaxy Tab S9 FE** is designed to provide a smooth and efficient user experience, there may be times when you encounter issues or performance slowdowns. Whether it's Wi-Fi connectivity problems, apps crashing, or poor battery life, understanding how to troubleshoot these common issues can help you resolve problems quickly and get your device back on track. Additionally, performing regular maintenance on both the hardware and software of your tablet ensures that it stays in optimal condition for years to come.

This chapter will guide you through troubleshooting common issues, performing a factory reset when necessary, and maintaining your tablet's hardware and software. By following these guidelines, you can keep your Samsung Galaxy Tab S9 FE running smoothly and prevent potential problems before they arise.

Common Issues and Fixes

When you encounter a problem with your tablet, it can often be frustrating, especially if you rely on it for work, communication, or entertainment. Fortunately, many issues have simple solutions that can be resolved without professional assistance. Below are some of the most common issues users face with the Samsung Galaxy Tab S9 FE, along with their fixes.

1. Wi-Fi Connectivity Issues

Wi-Fi issues are among the most common problems faced by tablet users. If you're having trouble connecting to a Wi-Fi network or experiencing a slow or unstable connection, there are several troubleshooting steps you can try.

Fixes for Wi-Fi Connectivity Issues:

- **Restart the Tablet and Router:**
    - The first step in resolving Wi-Fi issues is to restart your Galaxy Tab S9 FE and your router. This can often clear up temporary connectivity issues.
    - To restart your tablet, press and hold the **Power** button and select **Restart**. For your

117

router, unplug it for about 30 seconds, then plug it back in.

- **Forget and Reconnect to the Network:**

  o If your tablet isn't connecting to a specific Wi-Fi network, go to **Settings** > **Connections** > **Wi-Fi**. Tap on the **network name** and select **Forget**. Then, reconnect to the network by entering the Wi-Fi password again.

- **Check for Interference:**

  o Wi-Fi performance can be affected by physical obstructions or interference from other electronic devices. Try moving closer to the router or ensuring there's minimal interference from other devices, such as microwaves or cordless phones.

- **Reset Network Settings:**

  o If the issue persists, resetting the network settings can help resolve connection problems. Go to **Settings** > **General Management** > **Reset** > **Reset Network Settings**. This will reset all Wi-Fi, mobile data, and Bluetooth settings, so you'll need to reconnect to your networks afterward.

- **Update Router Firmware:**

  o Ensure that your router's firmware is up to date. Check the manufacturer's website or app for instructions on updating the router's firmware. Sometimes, outdated firmware can cause connectivity issues.

2. App Crashes and Freezing

It's not uncommon for apps to freeze or crash unexpectedly, especially when your device's memory or processing power is under stress. There are a variety of reasons apps might crash, including outdated software, insufficient memory, or software conflicts.

Fixes for App Crashes and Freezing:

- **Restart the App:**

  o If an app crashes or freezes, try restarting it. Close the app by tapping the **Recent Apps** button (the square icon) and swiping away the app you want to close. Then, reopen the app to see if the issue persists.

- **Clear App Cache:**

  - Cached data can sometimes interfere with the app's performance. To clear the cache for an app, go to **Settings** > **Apps** > **[App Name]** > **Storage**, then tap **Clear Cache**. This will not delete any app data but will remove temporary files.

- **Update the App:**

  - App updates often include bug fixes and performance improvements. Open the **Google Play Store** or **Samsung Galaxy Store**, search for the app, and check for any available updates. If there is an update, install it and see if it resolves the issue.

- **Reinstall the App:**

  - If the app continues to crash, try uninstalling it and reinstalling it. Go to **Settings** > **Apps** > **[App Name]**, then tap **Uninstall**. After the app is uninstalled, reinstall it from the Play Store or Galaxy Store.

- **Check for System Updates:**

  o Sometimes, app crashes are due to compatibility issues with the operating system. To check for system updates, go to **Settings** > **Software Update** > **Download and Install**.

3. Poor Battery Life

If you notice that your tablet's battery drains quickly, there are several factors to consider. High screen brightness, background apps, and power-hungry apps can all contribute to reduced battery performance.

Fixes for Poor Battery Life:

- **Enable Battery Saver Mode:**

  o **Battery Saver Mode** reduces the tablet's background activity and dims the screen to conserve power. To activate it, go to **Settings** > **Battery and Device Care** > **Battery** > **Power Saving Mode**. Choose between **Medium Power Saving** and **Maximum Power Saving** based on your needs.

- **Reduce Screen Brightness:**

o   The screen is one of the biggest consumers of battery. To save power, reduce the screen brightness by swiping down on the notification panel and adjusting the brightness slider.

- **Disable Background Apps:**

  o   Apps running in the background can consume battery life, even when you're not actively using them. To close apps, tap the **Recent Apps** button and swipe away the apps you no longer need.

- **Turn Off Unnecessary Features:**

  o   Disable features like **Bluetooth**, **GPS**, and **Wi-Fi** when not in use. These can drain battery life if left on unnecessarily. You can quickly toggle these features off from the notification panel.

- **Check Battery Usage:**

  o   Go to **Settings** > **Battery and Device Care** > **Battery** > **Battery Usage**. This will show you a breakdown of which apps and services are consuming the most power. Consider uninstalling or restricting apps that use excessive battery life.

Factory Reset

A factory reset can be a helpful solution if your tablet is experiencing significant issues, such as constant crashes, freezing, or sluggish performance that cannot be fixed with other troubleshooting methods. However, before performing a factory reset, it's important to **back up your data** to avoid losing personal information, such as photos, contacts, and documents.

How to Back Up Your Data

Before performing a factory reset, ensure you back up important data, such as contacts, apps, messages, photos, and videos. Samsung offers several ways to back up your data:

Using Samsung Cloud:

1. **Open Settings:**

   o Go to **Settings > Accounts and Backup**.

2. **Select Samsung Cloud:**

   o Tap **Samsung Cloud**, then select **Backup and Restore**.

123

3. **Back Up Your Data:**

   o Tap **Back Up Data**, choose the data types you want to back up (e.g., contacts, messages, apps), and tap **Back Up**.

Using Google Backup:

1. **Open Settings:**

   o Go to **Settings** > **Accounts and Backup**.

2. **Select Backup:**

   o Tap **Google Backup**, then toggle **Back Up to Google Drive** to ON.

3. **Back Up Your Data:**

   o Ensure your contacts, app data, and other important files are backed up to your Google account.

Once your data is safely backed up, you can proceed with a factory reset.

How to Perform a Factory Reset

If your Galaxy Tab S9 FE is still experiencing issues after troubleshooting, performing a **factory reset** may be necessary. This will erase all data on the tablet, so it's important to back up your files first.

1. **Open Settings:**

   o Go to **Settings** > **General Management**.

2. **Select Reset:**

   o Tap **Reset**, then choose **Factory Data Reset**.

3. **Review Reset Information:**

   o You'll see a list of accounts and data that will be erased during the reset. Make sure everything is backed up.

4. **Confirm Reset:**

   o Tap **Reset** and then **Delete All** to begin the factory reset process. Your tablet will restart and begin the reset. This may take a few minutes.

5. **Set Up Your Tablet:**

   o After the reset is complete, your tablet will boot up as if it were new. You can now restore your data from your backup and set up the device as you wish.

Maintenance Tips

Regular maintenance is essential for keeping your Galaxy Tab S9 FE in good working condition. Both the hardware and software of the tablet require attention to ensure optimal performance, longevity, and security.

1. Cleaning the Screen and Body

Dirt, fingerprints, and smudges can accumulate on your tablet's screen and body, affecting the display quality and making it harder to use the device. Proper cleaning helps maintain a clear, smudge-free screen and prevents long-term damage.

How to Clean the Screen:

1. **Turn Off the Tablet:**

    o   Power off your Galaxy Tab S9 FE to prevent accidental touches on the screen during cleaning.

2. **Use a Microfiber Cloth:**

    o   Use a soft **microfiber cloth** to gently wipe the screen. Avoid using paper towels or abrasive cloths, as they may scratch the screen.

3. **Dampen the Cloth if Necessary:**

   o If needed, lightly dampen the microfiber cloth with water or a screen-safe cleaner. Do not apply the liquid directly to the screen.

4. **Clean the Body:**

   o Wipe the back and sides of the tablet with the microfiber cloth to remove any dirt or fingerprints.

2. Keeping Software Up to Date

Regular software updates are essential for maintaining security, fixing bugs, and improving performance. Ensure that your tablet is always running the latest software version to take advantage of new features and improvements.

How to Check for Updates:

1. **Open Settings:**

   o Go to **Settings** > **Software Update**.

2. **Check for Updates:**

   o Tap **Download and Install** to check if there are any available updates. If an update is available, follow the on-screen prompts to install it.

3. Uninstall Unused Apps

Over time, you may accumulate apps that you no longer use. These apps take up storage space and can potentially slow down your device. Regularly uninstalling unused apps helps keep your tablet running smoothly.

How to Uninstall Apps:

1. **Open Settings:**

   o Go to **Settings** > **Apps**.

2. **Select the App:**

   o Find the app you want to uninstall, tap on it, then tap **Uninstall**.

3. **Confirm the Uninstallation:**

   o Confirm the action to uninstall the app. This will free up storage space and improve performance.

Troubleshooting and maintenance are essential practices to ensure your **Samsung Galaxy Tab S9 FE** continues to perform at its best. Whether you're dealing with Wi-Fi connectivity issues, app crashes, or poor battery life, most common problems can be solved with simple steps. In more severe cases, performing a factory reset may be necessary to restore your device to its optimal state.

Regular maintenance, such as cleaning the screen, updating software, and managing storage by uninstalling unused apps, will also help extend the life of your tablet and maintain peak performance. By following the tips and troubleshooting techniques outlined in this chapter, you can keep your Galaxy Tab S9 FE running smoothly and efficiently for years to come.

CONCLUSION

Maximizing Your Samsung Galaxy Tab S9 FE

The Samsung Galaxy Tab S9 FE stands as one of the most versatile tablets in the market today, catering to a diverse range of users who need a reliable, powerful, and cost-effective device. From students, professionals, and creatives to casual users, the Galaxy Tab S9 FE offers something for everyone. Whether you are using it to enhance your productivity, stay connected with loved ones, create art, or enjoy entertainment on the go, this tablet can seamlessly integrate into your daily life and exceed expectations.

Throughout this user guide, we have explored every aspect of the Samsung Galaxy Tab S9 FE—from the initial setup and customization to the best practices for maintaining its performance and battery life. In the following sections, we will recap some of the tablet's key features and the insights shared in this guide, underscoring why the Samsung Galaxy Tab S9 FE is a remarkable investment for users looking for a feature-rich yet affordable tablet.

A Powerful Tablet with Versatile Features

One of the defining aspects of the Samsung Galaxy Tab S9 FE is its impressive range of features that make it highly adaptable to different user needs. The tablet's robust performance, equipped with a capable processor and a fluid display, makes it an ideal choice for both professional and recreational activities. Whether you're running multiple apps simultaneously, editing documents, streaming media, or indulging in your favorite mobile games, the tablet offers a smooth and responsive experience.

Productivity Tools such as Samsung DeX, S Pen support, and seamless app integration allow users to transform the tablet into a portable workstation. With Samsung DeX, you can turn your tablet into a desktop-like experience, using multiple windows for multitasking, while the S Pen brings precision and creativity for note-taking, sketching, and annotating documents. These tools make the Galaxy Tab S9 FE an ideal choice for those who need both entertainment and productivity capabilities.

Impressive Display and Design

The display of the Galaxy Tab S9 FE offers vibrant colors, sharp resolution, and a smooth refresh rate, making it perfect for media consumption, gaming, and productivity. Whether you're watching your favorite shows on streaming platforms or editing high-quality images, the tablet's high-resolution screen ensures that every detail is crisp and clear. The adaptive display features, including options for blue light filters and refresh rate adjustments, further enhance the viewing experience.

Additionally, the tablet's lightweight design and sleek build make it easy to carry around, whether you're working at the office, attending classes, or traveling. The premium design is not only visually appealing but also built for durability, ensuring that it stands up to everyday use.

Customization and Ease of Use

The Samsung Galaxy Tab S9 FE offers a high level of customization, allowing users to adjust their settings according to their preferences. From the lock screen, themes, wallpapers, and font size to configuring accessibility settings for ease of use, you can make the tablet truly your own. The One UI operating system enhances the tablet's intuitive interface, allowing you to easily navigate through menus, notifications, and apps.

In addition to aesthetics, the app organization features, including folders and the split-screen mode, make it easier to keep your apps and tasks organized. The split-screen mode further enhances multitasking capabilities by allowing users to run two apps side by side, boosting efficiency when working or interacting with content.

Security and Privacy Features

When it comes to security and privacy, the Galaxy Tab S9 FE provides robust features that ensure your data and personal information are protected. The tablet includes multiple biometric authentication options, such as fingerprint scanning and facial recognition, allowing you to securely access your device without compromising convenience. These biometric systems make it harder for unauthorized users to gain access to your device, keeping your files and data safe.

The tablet also integrates Samsung Knox, a comprehensive mobile security platform that offers encryption, real-time monitoring, and protection against malware and other security threats. With Find My Device, users can easily track their tablet if it gets lost, and with regular software updates, your device stays secure from emerging security vulnerabilities.

Performance and Battery Optimization

One of the major advantages of the Samsung Galaxy Tab S9 FE is its performance, ensuring a smooth experience even during heavy use. By following the tips shared in this guide for performance optimization—such as managing apps, disabling unused apps, and clearing cache—you can keep the tablet running at its best for extended periods of time. Performance optimization ensures that apps run efficiently, reducing slowdowns and improving response times for a better overall experience.

For battery life, the Galaxy Tab S9 FE offers several ways to improve energy efficiency. By using features like Battery Saver Mode, reducing screen brightness, limiting background apps, and managing connectivity features like Bluetooth and Wi-Fi, you can extend your tablet's battery life to get through the day without needing to recharge. The tablet's long-lasting battery allows you to enjoy hours of work or entertainment, and by practicing battery-saving tips, you can get even more longevity out of each charge.

Keeping Your Device Updated

To ensure that your tablet remains up to date with the latest security features, bug fixes, and performance improvements, software updates are essential. The Samsung Galaxy Tab S9 FE provides a streamlined update process, enabling users to quickly check for and install updates. By keeping the software updated, you benefit from the latest advancements, ensuring that your tablet is always equipped with the best features available. This also helps improve device security, ensuring that you are protected from potential threats and vulnerabilities.

Troubleshooting and Maintenance

While the Samsung Galaxy Tab S9 FE is a highly reliable device, there may be occasions where you encounter issues that require troubleshooting. This guide has provided a detailed approach to common problems such as Wi-Fi connectivity issues, app crashes, and poor battery life. With simple fixes, such as restarting the device, clearing cache, and managing background apps, you can quickly address most of these concerns and restore your tablet to its optimal performance.

If you find that the tablet is not functioning as expected, a factory reset is a reliable last resort to resolve persistent problems. Before performing a factory reset, ensure that your data is properly backed up to avoid losing important files and information. Regular maintenance, such as cleaning

135

the screen, updating apps, and managing storage space, will also help keep your device running smoothly.

A Device Built to Last

The Samsung Galaxy Tab S9 FE is designed with durability in mind, and with the right care and maintenance, it can provide years of reliable service. The tablet's solid build quality, responsive performance, and long battery life make it an excellent choice for anyone in need of a dependable, versatile device. With regular updates, a bit of maintenance, and some simple troubleshooting tips, you can ensure that your Galaxy Tab S9 FE continues to perform at its best for years.

In conclusion, the Samsung Galaxy Tab S9 FE is a well-rounded device that delivers outstanding performance, versatility, and value. From its powerful hardware and intuitive interface to its extensive productivity tools and robust security features, the tablet provides everything you need to stay productive, creative, and entertained. By following the advice and tips provided in this user guide, you can maximize the tablet's capabilities and ensure that it continues to serve your needs for the long term.

Whether you're using it for work, school, entertainment, or creativity, the Galaxy Tab S9 FE is an excellent choice for anyone looking for a high-quality tablet at an affordable price. Its combination of features, performance, and value make it a standout in its category. By maintaining the tablet properly, optimizing its performance, and keeping the software updated, you can enjoy a seamless user experience and get the most out of your device for years to come.

www.ingramcontent.com/pod-product-compliance
Lightning Source LLC
LaVergne TN
LVHW051654050326
832903LV00032B/3800